Explore Dorset Abbeys and Churches

by Robert Westwood

Inspiring Places Publishing
2 Down Lodge Close
Alderholt
Fordingbridge
Hants
SP6 3JA

www.inspiringplaces.co.uk

ISBN 978-0-9955964-1-2

Inspiring places

JURASSIC COAST QUALITY BUSINESS

Contents

Carving on a misericord, Sherborne Abbey.

Introduction

It is easy to forget what a wonderful heritage of medieval buildings we have in our country's churches. The rural county of Dorset is blessed with a fine collection; the earliest date from Saxon times while many were built or substantially altered in the thirteenth, fourteenth and fifteenth centuries. Before the Dissolution of the Monasteries under Henry VIII, Dorset's fertile acres supported many prosperous abbeys and priories where magnificent churches were at the centre of vast estates. Although these buildings were often plundered and stone taken for later buildings, evocative remains are still to be found, sometimes cared for by estates that were acquired by wealthy lords and civil servants loyal to the king. Others were luckier, churches were sometimes handed over to the locals to be used as parish churches. Away from the centres of the grand monastic estates much humbler places of worship were built for the villages. Many of these were later enlarged and 'improved' through bequests from wealthy landowners, but a few very small, plain churches remain, all the more charming for their simplicity and the beauty of their surroundings.

Very many of Dorset's churches and abbeys are well worth a visit; the ones featured in this book are a personal choice and there are others that could have been included and which other people might have. Some are in stunning locations, many have wonderful architectural or decorative features while some have particularly interesting stories associated with them. This is a guide for those who want to escape the madding crowd and find special places, perhaps to find peace and tranquility in a beautiful location or to enjoy and appreciate exquisite artistry.

Windows in St Nicholas's Church, Moreton..

St Candida and Holy Cross, Whitchurch Canonicorum

There are said to be only two churches in the whole of England that contain the remains of a saint; one is Westminster Abbey (Edward the Confessor), the other is the church of St Candida and Holy Cross at Whitchurch Canonicorum. Known as the 'Cathedral of the Vale' (Marshwood Vale), this beautiful church was begun in the reign of William the Conqueror and was greatly enlarged in 1190. The first mention of the church is in 881 when Alfred the Great bequeathed the manor to his youngest son. The name 'Whitchurch' may derive from that of the saint (Candida is Latin for white) or possibly from the light coloured stone. The saint herself is a mysterious figure; one story suggests she was a Saxon princess and recluse who lived on the cliffs and lit beacons for sailors. She was tortured (losing a finger) and possibly murdered by Danish raiders at nearby Charmouth but managed to warn the villagers who were able to escape to a safe place. However, the Reverend S. Baring-Gould suggested she may be Gwen, the daughter of a prince of Brittany in the fifth century, who married twice and was the mother of two saints. There are a number of churches dedicated to her in Brittany and when, in the reign of Athelstan, many people from Brittany sought refuge in England, Athelstan allowed them to settle in parts of Wessex. They brought with them sacred relics and it may be that the king gave these to the church here partly because of the name; Gwen is a Celtic name associated with white.

One story from Brittany tells of Gwen captured by pirates, but later escaping after losing two fingers from an axe blow.

A shrine to Saint Candida (or Wyte/Wite) is to be found in an alcove in the north transept of the church. Its lower part looks like a tomb with three elliptical holes, through which people put diseased limbs or letters to the saint, hoping for their injuries and illnesses to be healed. On top of this is a stone reliquary which, in 1850, was found to contain the bones of a small woman, intriguingly missing a finger. When it was opened again in 1900 an inscription was found saying (in Latin) 'Here lie the bones of St Wite'. So, it may well be that there are really two churches in England that hold the remains of a saint; certainly people still ask the saint for help, as any visitor can see from the notes left in the shrine today.

Pg 4: The shrine of St Wite in the church.
Above: The church of St Candida and Holy Cross.
Right: Statue of St Wite on south wall of church.

Practical Information:
Whitchurch Canonicorum near Bridport, signed from A35, DT6 6RJ.
Open daily 10am to 4pm.

Forde Abbey

In 1133 a wealthy nobleman, Richard de Brioniis, built a priory on his land in Devon and invited Cistercian monks from Waverley Abbey to found a new community there. Unfortunately, the land was not particularly fertile but the project was saved when his sister and successor Adelicia gave the monks a new parcel of land in Dorset. The monks' new home was near an ancient river crossing and soon became known as Forde Abbey. As befits such an idyllic site, the abbey grew, prospered and enjoyed a relatively trouble free existence until it was peacefully handed over to the commissioners of

Forde Abbey, set in beautiful gardens.

Henry VIII in 1539. In fact it was so prosperous that it eventually owned and managed around 30 000 acres of rich agricultural land.

Since the Dissolution the abbey has been occupied by a number of individuals and families, but from the beginning of the twentieth century has been in the care of the Roper family who have expanded and improved the delightful gardens which were established in the eighteenth century. The abbey church no longer exists but there are still some monastic parts that remain, including the Great Hall. Forde Abbey has long been a magnificent country home rather than a religious house but its setting does give some idea of the fabulous wealth and resources of the grand abbeys.

Practical Information:
4 miles south-east of Chard, Somerset, TA20 4LU. fordeabbey.co.uk
Open: Gardens every day 10am to 5:30pm, house 2 April - 31 October, Tuesday to Friday and Sunday plus Bank Holiday Mondays. (2017 times, please check on website.)
Dogs welcome on leads in gardens. Entrance fee.

Abbotsbury Abbey and St Nicholas' Church

Golden Jurassic limestone has been a major factor in creating some of England's most picturesque towns and villages, and Abbotsbury certainly fits in this category. As the name suggests, it was once dominated by a large Benedictine abbey, founded in the 1040s by a Scandinavian named Orc, who had been a thegn of King Canute. It quickly prospered and at some stage the monks started a swannery on the reed beds of the nearby Fleet lagoon. This institution has continued to the present day, although the swans are no longer used for food. The church of St Nicholas dates from the late fourteenth or early fifteenth century and was built to serve as the parish church of the village. It was situated next to the main abbey buildings, little of which remain. As you might expect, it was 'dissolved' in 1539 on the orders of Henry VIII who sold it to Sir Giles Strangways whose descendants have owned the estate ever since. In 1644 the village was the scene of fighting in the Civil War. Colonel James Strangways supported the king and used his manor house as a stronghold against a party of Parliamentarians. The struggle between the two sides spread to the church where two holes in the oak pulpit testify to the power of musket shot. The Strangways manor which stood next to the surviving wall of the abbey near the church was later deliberately destroyed by the Parliamentarians. The tower and north wall are the oldest parts of the church. In the porch is an effigy of an abbot thought to date from the late twelfth century, while just outside it are two medieval sarcophagi from the abbey, now used to plant flowers.

On the hill to the west of the abbey sits St Catherine's Chapel, probably built in the late fourteenth century. With spectacular views over Abbotsbury and the Fleet, it served as both a lookout and marker for ships off the coast. St Catherine is the patron saint of spinsters and a tradition developed that saw young women visit the chapel to pray for a husband.

St Catherine's Chapel is one of two buildings to survive the Dissolution, the other being the magnificent Tithe Barn. Built around 1400 it is over 270 feet long and is now, perhaps fittingly, home to a children's farm. Presumably these two buildings survived because of their usefulness, the others provided valuable stone for other constructions. If you walk from the church into the village, look out for remains of the abbey along the road, they might give you some idea of what a prosperous and extensive institution this once was.

Practical Information:
Abbotsbury, DT3 4JJ. Tithe Barn and St Catherine's can both be seen from the church and are a short walk away.

Pg 10: St Nicholas' Church.
Top: The Tithe Barn.
Bottom left: St Catherine's Chapel.
Bottom right: Bullet hole in pulpit.

St Mary the Virgin, Melbury Bubb

Lying not far from tiny St Edwold's (see next page), Melbury Bubb is another small church where the picturesque and tranquil setting makes a journey worthwhile. The first part of the parish's name comes from two Old English words meaning multi-coloured and fortified; presumably any fortification was on neighbouring Bubb Down Hill. The second part of the name may derive from a Saxon lord named Bubba. The tower of this small church is from the fifteenth century but the main part was rebuilt in 1854. Its simplicity complements the surroundings and its main treasure, a font carved out of part of what was a Saxon cross. The original cross probably marked a spot where preaching took place and so this may have a long history as a place of worship. The font carries a beautifully carved frieze of various animals and was turned upside down when the font was hollowed out. There can't be many places like this, next to a Jacobean manor house and at the end of a no through road, the church sits at the foot of a wooded hill. Inside there are no electric lights, only oil lamps on the walls, and the heating is provided by a small stove next to the entrance. The beauty of its surroundings and the simplicity of the church make it truly enchanting.

Practical Information:
7 miles south of Sherborne, DT2 0NQ. Open in daylight.

Left: The Saxon font in the church of St Mary the Virgin. Above: The church interior, note the stove by the door.

St Edwold's Church, Stockwood

The church of St Edwold at Stockwood is reputed to be the smallest in Dorset and one of the smallest in England, measuring roughly 9m by 4m. Its dedication is unique in Dorset and we meet St Edwold again at nearby Cerne Abbas; the brother of a Saxon king of East Anglia who became a recluse. It is unclear why this tiny church is dedicated to Edwold, it may be that he had a cell here too. The church itself dates from the fifteenth century with the porch added in 1636, but the name would suggest that a much earlier place of worship existed here. It sits beside a Georgian farmhouse at the foot of Bubb Down and is accessed by a path and small footbridge. Surrounded by trees and with a stream meandering past, it is another church worth seeing for its charming setting.

Practical Information:
Stockwood, DT2 0NG.
Open daily. Access via footbridge, parking at top of lane.

Above and left: Two views of the church.

The Isle of Portland

Accessed via a small path above Church Ope Cove on the east side of Portland, **St Andrew's Church** was the isle's first parish church and dates from the thirteenth century. Today it lies in ruins, abandoned in the mid-eighteenth century after a landslip left it in danger of collapse. It is a beautiful, peaceful spot with wonderful views out to sea. In the graveyard are one or two headstones carved with a skull and crossbones; this unusual feature, together with the church's situation have led some to speculate that these are the graves of pirates. However, although fairly unusual, this symbol was used merely to emphasise man's mortality. The church had quite a colourful history, in 1340 and 1404 it was torched by French raiders and rebuilt both times.

Another Portland church is dedicated to St Andrew; this is the **Avalanche Memorial Church**, also known as the Church of St Andrew. This simple church in Southwell, built in 1879, is a memorial to the SS Avalanche and the SS Forest, two ships that collided off Portland in a storm in 1877. One hundred and six people lost their lives and the church features

Practical Information:
St Andrew's - short walk off footpath to Church Ope Cove (signposted). DT5 1HS. St George's - Wide Street, Reforme, DT5 2JP. Open daily. Church of St Andrew - DT5 2EQ.

Above: The ruins of St Andrew's. Right: Skull and crossbones on a tomb.

This page top: St George's and graveyard. Bottom left: Carved headstone. Middle: Interior, showing box pews.

memorials to the victims and testaments to the bravery of local fishermen who brought them and the survivors to shore. The anchor of the Avalanche sits in the graveyard.

Situated in the centre of the isle near the villages of Easton and Weston is **St George's Church**, commissioned as the replacement parish church after it became obvious St Andrew's was no longer fit for purpose. It is a magnificent, monumental work designed by local mason Thomas Gilbert and built of local Portland Stone. The interior is beautifully preserved with its original, painted box pews. It is now in the care of the Churches Conservation Trust and open daily. The extensive graveyard has elaborate, carved Portland stone memorials and headstones telling stories of piracy and adventure. The grass is left deliberately long to encourage wildlife and helps create a wonderfully atmospheric setting.

Fleet Old Church

There is a remarkable story associated with this little church in its lovely secluded setting behind Chesil Beach. It all took place in the early hours of the morning of 23rd November 1824. It was then that a ferocious storm with hurricane force winds struck the south coast of England causing tremendous damage and much loss of life. The strong winds began on the evening of November 22nd and at 3am on the 23rd, at Lyme Regis, the sea was over a metre higher than it should have been, five hours before high tide. At 4am Weymouth's quays were inundated and at about the same time almost every house in Christchurch was flooded.

The sea was particularly high at Fleet, and one onlooker reported that it had nearly reached the top of Chesil Beach. Between 5am and 7am some exceptionally high waves struck the coast. At Fleet the sea began to break over the beach at 6am and a wave swept up the valley towards the church at a speed thought to be about 30mph. It demolished the nave and swept away five houses. One man saw the wave sweeping up the valley carrying a whole haystack on its crest. Today only the chancel of the church is left, the nave was completely destroyed. It is said the water reached a depth of around thirty feet here; a visit will give some appreciation of how devastating this storm must have been. A new church was later built for the villagers a little way inland.

Fleet Old Church.

Practical Information: Fleet Road, Chickerell, DT3 4EE. Park by new church in Fleet Road. Footpath signposted to old church.

St Michael's Church, Stinsford

Thomas Hardy's early masterpiece *Under the Greenwood Tree* is a pictorial depiction of Dorset rural life in Victorian times and concerns a group of church musicians in the small village of Mellstock. The model for this fictional settlement is considered to be Stinsford and St. Michael's, his Mellstock Church. A major theme in the story is the vicar's replacement of the musicians, who play at services in the musicians' gallery, with a modern organ, played by the schoolmistress, Fancy Day. Hardy's father played the fiddle in such a group of musicians in Stinsford Church and a gallery can still be seen there, although not the original. This was removed in Victorian times but a new one was installed in 1996, a gift from an American scholar, Richard Purdy.

The church itself is suitably ancient for such a literary role, mainly thirteenth century with a fourteenth century tower, although the nave roof was restored in the nineteenth century. Inside, in the south aisle, is a carving of St Michael in Ham Stone, thought to be late Saxon. This was Thomas Hardy's parish church which he attended as a boy and where he later taught at Sunday school. The cottage where he was born and lived until he married is a short distance away at Higher Bockhampton. Fittingly, his heart is buried in the churchyard along with his two wives and other family members; his ashes were interred in Poets' Corner, Westminster Abbey. The churchyard also contains the grave of another famous poet Cecil Day-Lewis, appointed Poet Laureate in 1968 and a big admirer of Hardy.

Practical Information: Stinsford near Dorchester, DT2 8PT.

Above left: St Michael's, Stinsford. Above right: The Hardy memorial window.

Sherborne Abbey

Aldhelm of Malmesbury was made the first Bishop of Sherborne in AD 705 after the bishopric of Winchester was split for ease of administration. A talented scholar, preacher and musician, Aldhelm travelled extensively around Dorset and founded a number of churches. His cathedral church was on the site of the present abbey and this became part of a Benedictine monastery when the bishopric was moved to Old Sarum in 1075. The abbey still has some Saxon features but the main church is Norman with extensive remodelling in the fifteenth century when the choir section was rebuilt in the Perpendicular style. It was at this time that the wonderful fan vaulting was completed, possibly the finest in England. The fan vaulting in the choir is perhaps even more beautiful than that of the nave and is around sixty years older. Sherborne continued as a monastery until 1539 when it was handed over to the commissioners of Henry VIII. The abbey church became the parish church and has remained so ever since.

Two Saxon kings of Wessex, Aethelbald and Ethelbert, both elder brothers of Alfred the Great, were buried here and two sarcophagi in the north choir aisle may contain their remains. The Lady Chapel contains an engraved glass reredos by Laurence Whistler (see Moreton Church). There are many other features of interest inside and outside this wonderful church; including fantastic gargoyles of dragons and beasts, beautifully carved corbels on the small towers to the left and right of the entrance porch, intricately carved capitals of pillars near the south door and charming carvings on the misericords ('mercy seats') in the choir.

Pg 16: The abbey church at Sherborne.
Top: The fan vaulting of the choir.
Bottom: Two of the wonderfully carved capitals on pillars near the south door.

Practical Information:
Sherborne Abbey, Sherborne, DT9 3LQ.
Open 8am to 4pm in winter, 8am to 6pm BST. sherborneabbey.com

Cerne Abbey

In 870 AD Edwold of East Anglia refused the crown previously worn by his brother King Edmund who had been killed by Viking invaders. Perhaps tired of constant violence he left to become a hermit. It appears he settled on the site of what would later become Cerne Abbey, possibly thanks to his discovery of a convenient spring there. Legend tells that he asked local shepherds where he could find water, rewarding them with silver pennies when they kindly showed him the spring. The 'Silver Well' as it is now called is still a location treasured by many and carefully maintained by the people of Cerne. It reputedly has healing properties and it is said to ensure good health if a newly born child is dipped in the water as it is touched by light from the rising sun.

Edwold was later canonised and it is probably due to him that a Benedictine monastery was founded here in 987 AD during the monastic revival under King Edgar. The abbey flourished and the village of Cerne Abbas grew around it. The Book of Cerne is a richly decorated Saxon text containing some bible translations, poems, prayers and hymns. Its provenance is uncertain but some additions to it originated in Cerne and it may have been kept there at some stage. However, Aelfric (955-1022), the first abbot of Cerne did produce an organised body of writings that continued to be widely used by clergy after the Norman Conquest.

Apart from being plundered by King Canute (who later endowed it), Cerne Abbey seems to have had a relatively uneventful history, although Queen Margaret of Anjou, wife of Henry VI, did seek sanctuary here after the Yorkist victory at the Battle of Barnet. Like many others the abbey closed in 1539 when it was peacefully surrendered to the king's commissioner, Sir John Tregonwell.

Also in Abbey Street is the church of **St Mary the Virgin**. It was built around 1300 by the abbey as a parish church for the villagers who had probably previously used the abbey church. It has some notable features including medieval wall paintings which, although now faded, allow us to imagine how brightly decorated medieval churches once were. Outside, on the tower above the west door, is a small carving of the Madonna and child (left), unusual in that such carvings did not generally survive the purges under Oliver Cromwell.

The Abbot's Porch.

The remains of the abbey are meagre but still captivating. The large house at the end of Abbey Street marks the position of the South Gate. At the back of this (open to visitors) stands the Guest House and the Abbot's Porch, both dating from the late fifteenth century. The porch was part of the lodging for Abbot Thomas Sam, who it is thought lived above the entrance. The Silver Well can be found at the end of the path alongside the graveyard next to South Gate House.

Practical Information: The abbey is at the end of Abbey Street, Cerne Abbas, DT2 7JQ. The Silver Well is at the end of the churchyard near the abbey. St Mary's is also in Abbey Street.

St Andrew's Church, Melcombe Horsey (or Melcombe Bingham)

Charmingly and confusingly the church lies a short distance to the east of the village of Melcombe Bingham, also known as Melcombe Horsey, at Bingham's Melcombe. Faint outlines of a deserted medieval village immediately to the south of the church are visible from the air. The charming flint and stone fourteenth century church of St Andrew owes its place in this book to its setting; if ever there was a place that exemplifies an image of rural beauty and tranquility, this is it. The church can be accessed via the driveway, also a public footpath, that leads to the delightful manor house (Bingham's Melcombe). The present house dates mainly from the sixteenth century but has been occupied since the thirteenth century. It was in the hands of the Bingham family for around six hundred years until it was sold in 1895. Robert de Bingham acquired the manor in 1273 after his marriage to Lucy Turberville, a Dorset family that became famous through Thomas Hardy's heroine Tess.

Nestling in a little bowl between chalk hills, and with a stream bubbling past the church, this truly is a beautiful place. Take your time, wander down the path and around the churchyard, and perhaps sit a while in the sun on the little bench outside the church.

Above: The lovely setting of St Andrew's.

Practical Information: Near Melcombe Bingham (or Horsey), DT2 7PZ.

St Mary the Virgin, Puddletown

Puddletown was Thomas Hardy's 'Weatherbury' in *Far from the Madding Crowd* and St Mary's the scene of the marriage of Bathsheba and Gabriel Oak. This lovely, historic church dates from the twelfth century but most of what we see today is a fifteenth century rebuild. Inside are some wonderful features, notably a twelfth century Norman font and marvellous seventeenth century woodwork that includes box pews, the pulpit, altar rail and a gallery.

The village and church have long been associated with the medieval manor of Athelhampton a short distance away. This was built by Sir William Martyn in 1485 and held by that family for four generations. The south transept of the church is known as the Athelhampton Chantry and contains several tombs of the Martyn family. Although identification of the effigies on the tombs is uncertain, one particular feature present on two of them points to the Martyn family. Unusually the feet of two of the armour clad figures rest on an ape, a figure of which is also included in the family's coat of arms. These figures show armour and clothing typical of the late fourteenth century, but the earliest effigy in the south west corner of the chantry is thought to date from around 1300.

Practical Information:
The Green, Puddletown, DT2 8SN. Open daily, usually 9am-5pm (4pm in winter).

Above left: St Mary the Virgin, Puddletown.
Top right: A tomb of the Martyn family.
Left: A view from the nave.

Milton Abbey

There can be few public schools with a more glorious setting than Milton Abbey School. The large, magnificent but half finished church beside the school was once the church of Milton Abbey, a Benedictine monastery founded in 964 by King Edgar. There had been an even earlier church here founded by Athelstan in 933. The abbey church burnt down in 1309 and building immediately began on the present structure, taking about one hundred years to reach its current size. Unfortunately, the nave was never built, but inside there is some elaborate vaulting and, in the south transept, lovely stained glass designed by the famous architect and artist Augustus Pugin. The huge marble monument is to Caroline Damer, wife of Lord Milton. On a hill about three hundred yards to the east of the church sits **St Catherine's Chapel**, built in the twelfth century as a pilgrims' chapel. An unusual flight of grass steps leads from the rear of the abbey to the chapel but these are not now used. However, the chapel can be reached via a short path from the road leading to the school and presents an impressive view over the abbey church and its wonderful setting.

The abbey had been sold off after the Dissolution, and in 1752 was bought by Joseph Damer. He had the grand mansion built which is now the school and, not liking the close proximity of the original village, had it demolished and constructed, half a mile away, the unique village of Milton Abbas with its rows of identical thatched houses. An interesting story about the church concerns a six year old boy named John Tregonwell, son of the then owner. In 1605 he fell sixty feet from the tower but survived thanks to his voluminous petticoats acting as a parachute. One wonders what a six year old was doing, unsupervised, at the top of the tower!

Practical Information: At Milton Abbey School, DT11 0BZ. Open Monday to Sunday 10am to 5pm. Visitors car parking at the school.

Pg22: Inside the abbey. Above: Milton Abbey from St Catherine's Chapel.

St Nicholas' Church, Moreton

Moreton is a tiny scattered village that seems to lack any real centre. The church, when viewed from a distance would appear to be unremarkable, rebuilt in 1776 in early Gothic Revival style. It is unusually enclosed in a circular churchyard which might suggest some sort of pre-Christian site. Go inside the church and you will immediately appreciate that this building is far from unremarkable. In 1940 a German bomber dropped a bomb which caused a great deal of damage, shattering almost all the windows. This was most likely a mistake; the bomber may have been trying to target the nearby airfield at Warmwell. Restoration began after the war and Laurence Whistler was invited to design the new windows. The effect is stunning, the etched glass in the windows lets light flood in and the varied and intricate designs are a delight, creating a truly unique atmosphere.

T. E. Lawrence lived nearby during his time at Bovington Camp and it was Moreton Church that held his funeral after he was tragically killed in a motorbike accident. He is buried in the small churchyard across the road.

Practical Information:
Moreton, DT2 8RH.
Open daily, 9am to 6pm (4pm in winter).

Above: The wonderful, light interior of Moreton Church.
Pg 25 top left: St Nicholas' Church, Moreton.
Pg 25 top right and below: Details from two of the many engraved windows.

Laurence Whistler (1912 – 2000) was a poet and artist who came to work solely on glass engraving. He was the younger brother of the famous artist Rex Whistler and was the first president of the British Guild of Glass Engravers. He completed the designs on every window of the small church over a period of about thirty years. One of the windows, on the east side, can only be seen from the outside and carries a rather sinister design, the figure of a man hanging from a tree, coins falling out of his hand. The figure represents Judas and Whistler offered this window as a gift, calling it 'the forgiveness window'. The representation startled and shocked the parishioners and they were reluctant to accept the window which languished in the Dorset County Museum for many years. It was only in 2014 that it was finally installed.

Tarrant Crawford and Tarrant Rushton

The valley of the little River Tarrant holds eight villages in the space of ten miles, all named after the river. In medieval times there were nine churches of which seven survive. Visiting them all would be a rewarding experience but I have picked out two that I feel provide interesting and contrasting features.

Situated beside the River Tarrant and close to Tarrant Abbey Farm, the charming little church of **St Mary the Virgin, Tarrant Crawford** has a fascinating history and some interesting features. The abbey, another to be destroyed in the Reformation, was originally founded in 1186 and re-founded in 1228 by Richard Poore, the bishop responsible for the building of Salisbury Cathedral. It was a Cistercian nunnery and, at one time, possibly the richest in England. Buried somewhere here were the remains of Queen Joan, wife of Alexander II of Scotland and daughter of King John, allegedly in a golden coffin. The church may have been the lay church to the abbey and some of the neighbouring farm buildings were probably once part of this. It was built in the twelfth century; the chancel dates from this time but the nave and tower are fourteenth century. It is now redundant and looked after by the Churches Conservation Trust.

The interior of the church is quite plain but there are some wonderful and unusually extensive medieval wall paintings. These were completed in the fourteenth century and on the south wall is a series telling the story of St Margaret of Anjou. The lovely setting, the intriguing history and the wall paintings make a visit here a memorable experience.

Above left: St Mary's, Tarrant Crawford. Above right: Detail of the wall paintings. Pg 27 top: St Mary's, Tarrant Rushton. Below left: Acoustic aids. Below right: The leper window with finger marks.

Practical Information: Tarrant Crawford, take track by Tarrant Abbey Farm, DT11 9HU. Open daily, unlocked. Tarrant Rushton, DT11 8SD.

The little church of **St Mary's, Tarrant Rushton** is at the end of a quiet lane and is unusual in having a cruciform plan. It was first built in the mid twelfth century; much of the nave dates from this time but the rest is largely fourteenth century. Apart from being an extremely pretty church, both inside and out, it has a number of intriguing features. Set inside and on either side of the chancel arch are two earthenware jars, placed there in the fifteenth century as acoustic aids. They were thought to help the congregation better hear the priest but it is doubtful they make any difference. Also in the chancel arch are two hagioscopes or squints. These are openings at seated eye level to help people sitting in the aisles to see the high altar. Finally, in the north wall of the chancel, is the 'Leper Squint', a window designed to allow lepers outside the church to see the altar. There was a leper hospital nearby but they were not allowed into the church. In the sandstone surround of the window are marks thought to have been made by the fingers of lepers as they struggled to see what was going on inside the church.

Knowlton Church

Often cited as one of the most atmospheric places in Dorset, Knowlton Church is certainly unusual in that it sits inside a pagan Neolithic henge monument that was constructed around 2500 BC. The henge is an almost circular earth bank roughly one hundred metres in diameter and nearly two metres high. Inside the bank is a ditch two metres wide and around a metre deep. It was once part of a major Neolithic and Bronze Age ceremonial centre and the traces of a number of other henges are visible from aerial photographs. A number of burial barrows are also nearby, including the largest round barrow in Dorset. The church, now in ruins, was started in the twelfth century and added to over the years; the tower dates from the fifteenth century. It once served the village of Knowlton which lay to the west near the River Allen. Only faint traces of this now survive; it is thought to have been abandoned after the Black Death. The church continued to be used however and was only abandoned in the eighteenth century when the roof fell in.

It is not clear why a Christian place of worship was built inside a Neolithic henge but its setting with three hundred and sixty degree views of the beautiful Dorset countryside make it a unique spot. Many people come here to wander around and sit quietly and many leave messages for loved ones in a secluded grove by a yew tree. Unsurprisingly a number of legends have grown up around this place but you don't need to be aware of any of these to savour its special atmosphere.

Knowlton Church.

Practical Information: On minor road off B3078, signposted 'Bockhampton'. Open access at all times. BH21 5AE.

All Saints' Church, Chalbury

At about 330 feet above sea level on the edge of the Chalk downs and overlooking the valley of the River Allen, All Saints' Church, Chalbury perhaps occupies one of the loveliest positions of any church in Dorset. It is the parish church of the tiny village of Chalbury; the name is Old English and derives from 'Ceol's fort'. This may well have been a sacred spot well before Saxon times. It originally belonged to the Wilton Estate and was granted to the first Earl of Pembroke, the legendary knight William Marshall, at the beginning of the thirteenth century. The church dates from this time and still reflects its original simple, single-cell plan, consisting of just a nave, chancel and south porch, although it once also had a tower. Its position is so commanding that at one time a giant elm tree in the churchyard was used as a marker by shipping in the Channel. Sadly it is no longer there.

The plain whitewashed exterior with red tiled roof seems to complement its position perfectly, but it is the interior that is particularly appealing, a completely unaltered Georgian design with charming box pews painted in two-tone pastel colours. The pews are of different sizes, reflecting the relative status of the intended occupants.

Above: All Saints' Church, Chalbury.
Left: The lovely interior with box pews.

Practical Information: At Chalbury near Wimborne, BH21 7EY.

St James' Church, Kingston

The little Purbeck village of Kingston has two churches, one is now a private home while the other is a magnificent Gothic Revival style building designed by the famous Victorian architect George Street. This was commissioned in 1874 by John Scott, 3rd Earl of Eldon who lived at nearby Encombe House. It is not entirely clear why this second church was built but it certainly provided much work for local people in a time of recession. It was constructed of Purbeck Stone quarried on the Earl's estate and no expense was spared. For around forty years the other church continued to be the parish church and St James' was effectively a private chapel for the Eldon family. However, in 1921 Lord Eldon gave it to the Church Commissioners and it became the new parish church.

It perhaps seems much too large and grand for the tiny village it serves, but it has become a Purbeck landmark and is a testament to the skill of local craftsmen who built it. The interior is just as grand as the outside with Purbeck Marble used extensively. There are richly carved capitals on the columns, contemporary stained glass windows and a huge rose window on the west wall.

Above: The nave and rose window. Pg 31 top: St James' Church. Bottom left: A carved capital. Bottom right: Intricate carving in Purbeck marble.

Practical Information: Kingston, near Wareham, BH20 5LL.

St John the Baptist, Bere Regis

Bere Regis gets the last part of its name from the fact that the Crown held the manor there from Saxon times until 1259 when it was granted to Simon de Montfort. King John is recorded as having visited sixteen times. In the thirteenth century it came into the hands of the Norman family perhaps synonymous with the village, the Turbervilles, immortalised by Thomas Hardy's *Tess of the D'Urbervilles*. The story centres around the fact that Tess' father John Durbeyfield believes he is a descendant of the ancient family. The real family held the manor at Bere Regis for around five hundred years but the line had died out by 1780. As might be expected they have left their mark in the church, under the south aisle of which is a large crypt containing the tombs of many of the Turbervilles. Windows in the south aisle show the coats of arms of those who have held manorial rights here, again, many of them from the Turberville family.

The earliest bits of the church date from late Saxon times but the main parts are twelfth and thirteenth century. The tower was added in the sixteenth century. The main glory of the church is the carved oak roof, given in 1485 by Cardinal Morton. Morton was a local Dorset man who rose to become Archbishop of Canterbury and later Lord Chancellor under Henry VII. He gave the roof in memory of his mother, a member of the Turberville family. Among the many carvings of the roof twelve full length figures of the Apostles project from the sides. The pews in the nave feature delightful carvings on the ends, no two are the same; and there are more quaint carvings on the pillars on the south side of the nave.

Top left ; A pew end. Top right: One of the apostles. Two middle right: Carvings on pillars. Bottom left: The oak roof.

Practical Information:
Bere Regis, BH20 7HQ. Generally open 9am to 5pm. Note: Roof restoration may restrict opening during winter 2017/2018.

St Bartholomew's Church, Sutton Waldron

Sutton Waldron is a little village five miles south of Shaftesbury and a little north of Iwerne Minster. It sits on a spring line at the foot of the Chalk escarpment and has been on valued agricultural land since Saxon times. By the mid-nineteenth century its old church was in disrepair and the rector, Canon Anthony Huxtable, decided it should be demolished and a new church built. You may not be particularly fond of Victorian churches, but two in Dorset are worth going out of your way to visit. One is at Kingston on the Isle of Purbeck (page 30), the other is here at Sutton Waldron. Described by Sir John Betjemen as "one of the best and most lovely examples of Victorian architecture", it was designed by George Alexander and has a number of delightful gothic features such as the small flying buttresses on the spire.

As lovely as the exterior of the church is, it is the interior that is particularly stunning. It was designed by Owen Jones, a successful and innovative architect and designer who, amongst other things, was responsible for the design and layout of the Great Exhibition. He was much influenced by the Islamic world and his elaborate painted design is wonderful, serving as a potent reminder of what medieval painted churches must have looked like. The chancel floor is decorated with intricate, coloured tiles designed by Owen Jones' mentor, Augustus Pugin.

Above right: The painted roof. Below left: The nave and right: The chancel floor.

Practical Information: Sutton Waldron, DT11 8PB.

St Andrew's Church, Winterborne Tomson

You will not be disappointed if you take the trouble to find this simple little church, a rare example of a single celled Norman church from the twelfth century with an apsidal east end. The walls were raised a little at the beginning of the sixteenth century, the roof rebuilt and windows added, but the character of the church has not changed since its origin. Inside the wonderful oak box pews and gallery were built at the beginning of the eighteenth century, courtesy of William Wake, a local man who had risen to become Archbishop of Canterbury. It ceased to be used in 1896 but in 1929 the Society for the Preservation of Old Buildings restored it, using money made from the sale of manuscripts donated by Thomas Hardy, who reportedly loved the little building; partly because it represented the kind of simple place of worship used by the rural community before any grand alterations by wealthy patrons.

A visit can be an uplifting experience, especially if combined with one to the nearby church at Bere Regis (page 32). Both are lovely and the contrast particularly poignant.

Above: St Andrew's Church.
Left: The eighteenth century box pews.

Practical Information: Off A31, DT11 9HA. Open daily.

Worth Matravers

The purpose and origin of most churches and chapels is clear, but not so the tiny chapel dedicated to **St Aldhelm** on the headland of the same name on the Isle of Purbeck. This stout building of Purbeck stone, about thirty feet square was built in the late twelfth century and is clearly Norman in style. It is surrounded by a low, circular earthwork that is thought to be Christian in origin and so might have been one of a number of places of worship established around Dorset by St Aldhelm, the first Bishop of Sherborne in the early eighth century. It is not just its square shape that is unusual, it has just one window and one door and is supported by a very thick central pillar. It has been suggested that it might originally have been intended as a lookout over the treacherous race off St Aldhelm's Head, but one window is hardly suitable. In any case a chaplain is recorded as receiving payment there in the thirteenth century – perhaps it was some sort of chantry where a resident priest was required to pray for sailors. The chapel had fallen out of use and into disrepair by the seventeenth century but was restored and reopened in 1874 when weekly services were held by local coastguards. In 2005 on the thirteen hundredth anniversary of St Aldhelm's dedication as Bishop of Sherborne, a new altar stone was laid and consecrated by Rowan Williams, Archbishop of Canterbury.

Finally, a local legend should be mentioned. In the twelfth century it is said that a grieving father built the chapel after he had witnessed his daughter and her husband drown after being shipwrecked off St Aldhelm's Head. Whatever its origin, this is a charming little building in a spectacular setting.

St Aldhelm's Chapel. Note the one tiny window.

The church of **St Nicholas of Myra**, Worth Matravers is one of the oldest in Dorset; the nave, tower and windows date from around 1100 while the chancel was rebuilt at the beginning of the fourteenth century. It was restored in Victorian times by James Hicks of Dorchester, the architect to whom Thomas Hardy was apprenticed. Inside is a wonderful, carved Norman arch separating the nave from the chancel. There has been speculation that it was brought from another church as it seems too wide for this church, but there is no evidence for that. In the graveyard are the graves of Benjamin Jesty and his wife. Jesty was the first man to use inoculation to safeguard against disease. He injected his wife and son with some cow pox virus using a darning needle, correctly predicting that this would offer immunity against smallpox. He never publicised his efforts and was only later recognised as the pioneer of vaccination.

The central pillar, St Aldhelm's.

The Norman arch inside St Nicholas'.

St Nicholas', Worth Matravers.

Practical Information:
St Aldhelm's is at St Aldhelm's Head, SY961755. Walk from Renscombe car park at BH19 3LL. St Nicholas', Worth Matravers, BH19 3LQ.

The Minster Church of St Cuthburga, Wimborne

Wimborne's lovely Minster has a long and fascinating history. Most of the building dates from the twelfth century when a college for secular canons founded by Edward the Confessor in 1043 was rebuilt by the Normans. The church is dedicated to St Cuthburga, sister to the Saxon King Ine of Wessex, who founded a Benedictine abbey here. It has two towers and a rather variegated appearance due to the mixture of stone that was used; green and buff limestones contrast with red sandstone. A thirteenth century spire once sat atop the smaller tower but was destroyed in a storm around 1600.

The Minster has a number of unusual and intriguing features. The chained library sits in what was once the treasury. It lost its 'treasure' in the Dissolution and was converted to its present use in 1686 thanks to a donation by the Reverend William Stone. It now houses a collection of rare books, all chained to the shelves. It was one of the first public libraries in Britain and is still open to the public. On a wall of the west tower is the astronomical clock. The face of this lovely machine dates from the fourteenth century and the case is Elizabethan; the present workings were installed in 1792. The clock predicts the phases of the moon and the dial features the pre-Copernican view of the Earth at the centre of the universe. Perhaps the most unusual feature is the strange tomb seemingly set in a wall. Anthony Ettricke, a magistrate, fell out with church authorities and vowed never to be buried either inside or outside the church. He later made his peace with the church and this odd arrangement was made to allow him to keep his vow. Note the date on the tomb; this rather arrogant man was so sure of the year he would die he had it inscribed on the tomb beforehand. You might gather from the number that he was ten years out, succumbing in 1703 rather than 1693.

Pg 38: Anthony Ettricke's tomb, the 'man in the wall'. Top left: The Minster. Top right: The ceiling under the east tower. Middle right: The astronomical clock. Bottom: The nave and west window.

Practical Information: King Street, Wimborne, BH21 1EB. Open daily 9.30am to 5.30pm, March to Dec., 9.30am to 4pm Jan. and Feb. wimborneminster.org.uk

St Nicholas' Church, Studland

It was almost a thousand years ago that this lovely little church, aptly dedicated to the patron saint of sailors, merchants and repentant thieves, was built on the base of a former Saxon church. Now a popular, but still tranquil, beauty spot, Studland has witnessed invasions, piracy and smuggling as well as the ever busy legitimate traffic of traders and fishermen. It is well worth spending some time here to savour its atmosphere and appreciate its significant and somewhat surprising treasures.

This sturdy little building was constructed in Norman Romanesque style and has been little altered since; mostly by the addition of buttresses to counter the lack of a proper foundation. A variety of materials were used, some locally quarried stone and some that may have been left over from previous Saxon and Roman buildings. Inside the strong, curved chancel arches have been carved from local Purbeck stone with lovely decorations on the capitals of the supporting columns. In the Middle Ages the walls would have been plastered and intriguing remnants of medieval wall paintings survive but they were mostly removed in the Reformation.

Outside, where the roof joins the walls, you can see what is reputedly England's finest collection of corbels. Known as a 'corbel table' these carved roof supports come in a bewildering variety. Some are abstract shapes, some animals and some human figures. A few might seem outrageously vulgar for a church building (see pictures) but the church guide suggests they may have been intended as warning to an illiterate local population about the dangers of sexual excess.

Not to be missed is the grave of Sergeant Lawrence near the porch. The gravestone tells the remarkable story of this soldier who fought in many battles of the Napoleonic wars, including Waterloo. He met and married a French girl, retired to Studland where he kept a pub and 'lived happily ever after'.

Pg 40 top: St Nicholas' Church. Bottom left and right: Carved corbels. Above left: The nave and chancel arch from the chancel. Above top right: Carved capitals. Above bottom right: Traces of medieval frescoes.

Practical Information:
Near National Trust car park, South Beach, Studland, BH19 3AT.
Usually open daylight hours.

Christchurch Priory

Christchurch Priory has been called the most magnificent parish church in England, and at over three hundred feet it is certainly one of the longest. Originally an Augustinian priory, it was surrendered to the Crown in 1539. The priory buildings were demolished but the town successfully petitioned the king to allow them to keep the church.

A Norman church was begun here in the late eleventh century on the site of an earlier Saxon priory. Over the following centuries there were many new additions and alterations; in particular the thirteenth century saw the nave aisles vaulted and the clerestory built while the tower was rebuilt in the fifteenth century. The church has many wonderful features; some of the misericords date from the thirteenth century and are among the oldest in England; the Salisbury chantry completed in 1529 has superb fan vaulting and the fourteenth century stone reredos is equally spectacular. The priory also features lovely modern additions; in 1999 a new stained glass window was installed commemorating its nine hundredth anniversary.

Christchurch was originally called Twynham, but changed its name due to a lovely legend connected with the building work in the twelfth century. A workman cut a large and expensive oak beam too short. The work was abandoned for the night and when the builders returned the following morning the beam had been put in place and was the correct length. An unknown carpenter who had been seen on a few occasions earlier did not appear again and it was assumed to have been Christ and that he had performed the miraculous repairs. The 'Miraculous Beam' can be seen in the ambulatory.

Pg 42: The priory from across the harbour.
Top left: The priory tower and west end.
Top right: The reredos in the quire.
Above: A carving on one of the misericords.
Left: A detail of the quire reredos.

Practical Information:
Quay Road, Christchurch, BH21 1BU.
Open Monday to Saturday, 9.30am to 5pm, Sunday 2.15pm to 5.30pm.

St Martin's on the Walls, Wareham

The little church of St Martin's on the Walls is the most complete Saxon church in Dorset. Possibly founded by St Aldhelm, it is thought the early church may have been destroyed by Canute in 1015. The present building dates from 1030 and the nave and chancel are largely original. The 'wall' it stands on is part of the town's defences constructed on the orders of Alfred the Great to guard against the threat of Viking raids. The parish church of Wareham is the lovely Lady St Mary Church a short distance away beside the river. St Martin's was probably used by a small congregation on the north side of the town. It was abandoned in 1736 but restored in the early twentieth century and rededicated in 1936.

Inside are rare medieval frescoes, including, on the north wall of the chancel, one depicting St Martin of Tours and the legend of him cutting his cloak in two to give half to a naked beggar. Some red stars have been painted on another fresco and it is thought these may represent victims of the plague. Also in the church is a marble effigy of T. E. Lawrence (Lawrence of Arabia) sculpted by his friend Eric Kennington. Lawrence is clad in full Arab regalia and the sculpture was originally intended for St Paul's Cathedral. However, Lawrence's enthusiasm and admiration for Arab culture caused some consternation in official circles and St Paul's and a number of other churches (including Moreton, see page 24) refused to have it. St Martin's accepted it and it is perhaps fitting to Lawrence's dislike of public attention that it should end up in this charming little ancient place of worship.

Above left: St Martin's Church. Above right: Medieval frescoe of St Martin.

Practical Information:
North Street, Wareham, BH20 4AG. The church is usually locked but a key can be borrowed at A F Joy (outfitters) just down the road.

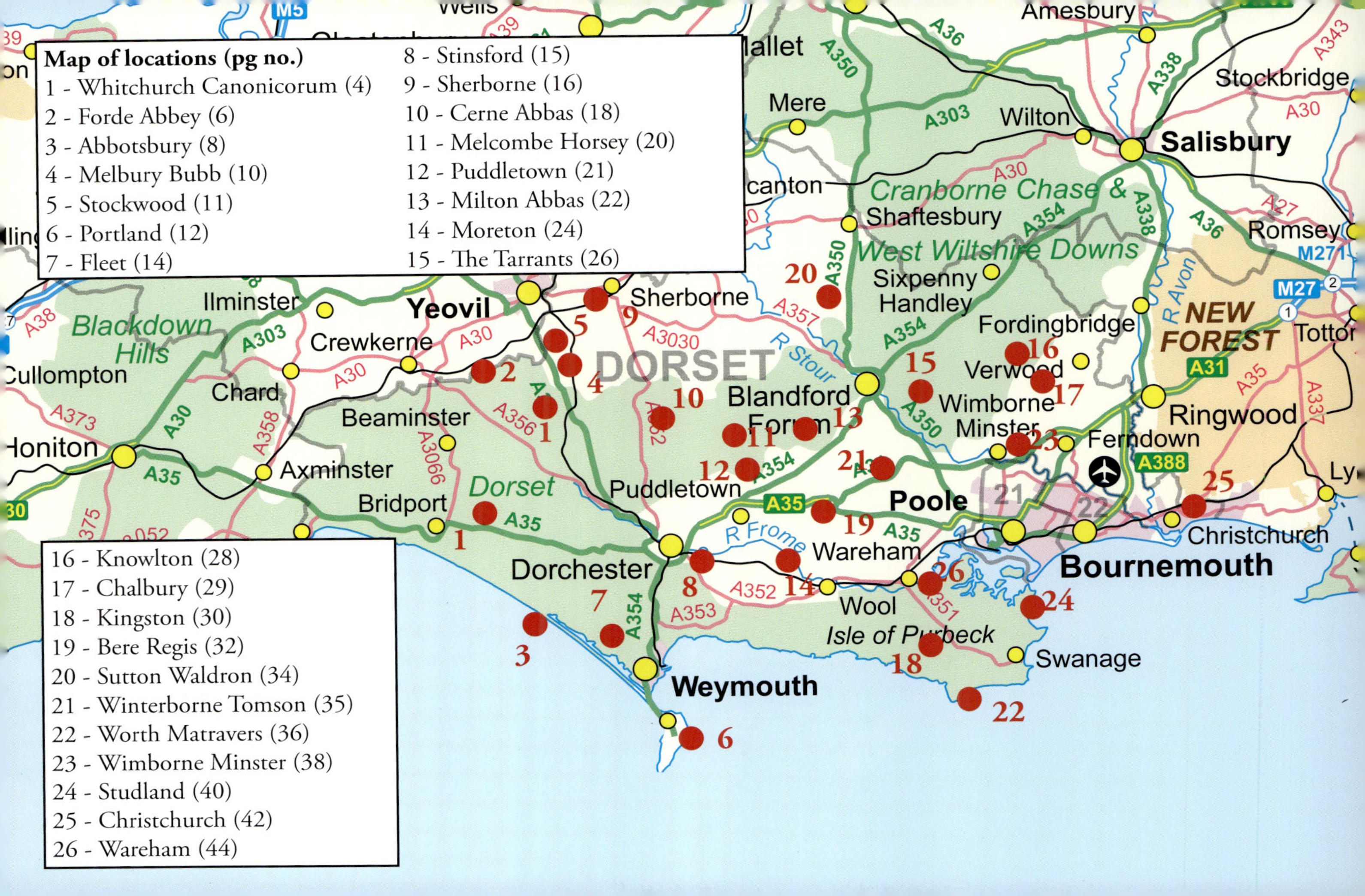
Map of locations (pg no.)
1 - Whitchurch Canonicorum (4)
2 - Forde Abbey (6)
3 - Abbotsbury (8)
4 - Melbury Bubb (10)
5 - Stockwood (11)
6 - Portland (12)
7 - Fleet (14)
8 - Stinsford (15)
9 - Sherborne (16)
10 - Cerne Abbas (18)
11 - Melcombe Horsey (20)
12 - Puddletown (21)
13 - Milton Abbas (22)
14 - Moreton (24)
15 - The Tarrants (26)
16 - Knowlton (28)
17 - Chalbury (29)
18 - Kingston (30)
19 - Bere Regis (32)
20 - Sutton Waldron (34)
21 - Winterborne Tomson (35)
22 - Worth Matravers (36)
23 - Wimborne Minster (38)
24 - Studland (40)
25 - Christchurch (42)
26 - Wareham (44)
DORSET
Salisbury
Amesbury
Stockbridge
Wilton
Mere
Shaftesbury
Romsey
Cranborne Chase &
West Wiltshire Downs
Sixpenny Handley
Fordingbridge
NEW FOREST
Ringwood
Verwood
Wimborne Minster
Ferndown
Christchurch
Bournemouth
Poole
Swanage
Isle of Purbeck
Wool
Wareham
Blandford Forum
Sherborne
Yeovil
Ilminster
Crewkerne
Chard
Blackdown Hills
Beaminster
Axminster
Honiton
Bridport
Dorset
Puddletown
Dorchester
Weymouth
R Stour
R Frome
R Avon

Glossary of church and architectural terms

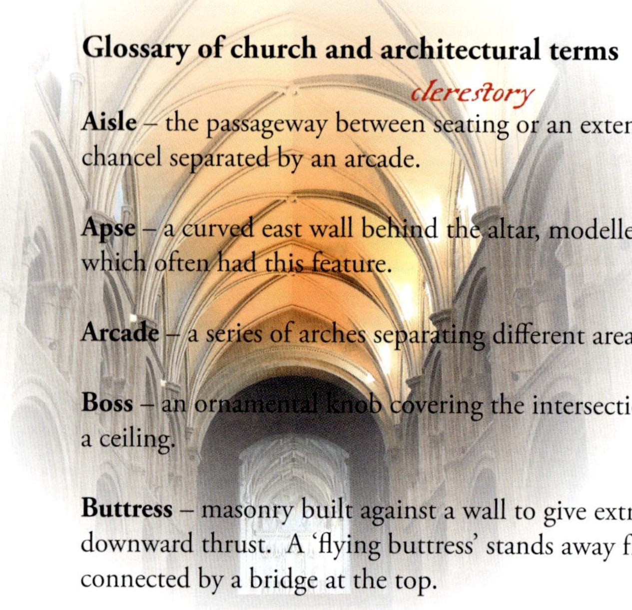

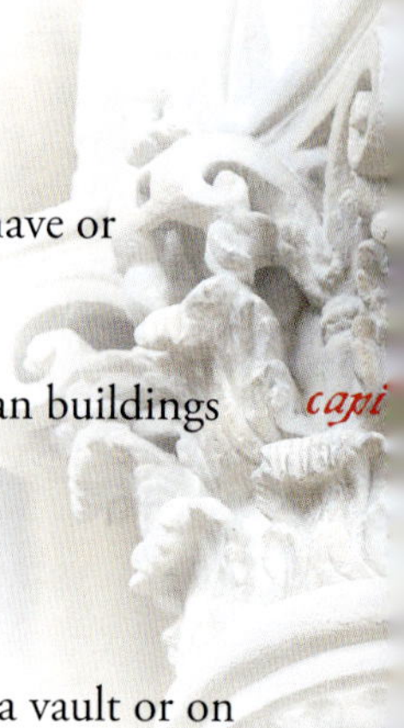

Aisle – the passageway between seating or an extension to the nave or chancel separated by an arcade.

Apse – a curved east wall behind the altar, modelled after Roman buildings which often had this feature.

Arcade – a series of arches separating different areas.

Boss – an ornamental knob covering the intersection of ribs in a vault or on a ceiling.

Buttress – masonry built against a wall to give extra strength and distribute downward thrust. A 'flying buttress' stands away from the wall and is connected by a bridge at the top.

Capital – the top part of a column, often decorated.

Chancel – the part of the church from which the service is conducted, usually three steps up from the nave. Often synonymous with sanctuary.

Chancel screen – see 'Rood screen'.

Chapel – in a large church an alcove with an altar or otherwise a smaller separate church.

Choir (or Quire) – the area where the choir sits.

Clerestory - the upper level of the nave, choir or transepts containing a series of windows.

Corbel – a block of stone on a wall supporting the end of a beam.

Crossing – the central part of a cruciform church.

Gallery – a balcony overlooking the main church.

Gargoyle – a grotesque carving or cast with a spout to divert water away from stonework.

Hagioscope (or Squint) – a small opening in a wall at eye level.

Misericord – a small shelf on the underside of a folding seat, designed to give relief when standing for long periods of prayer.

Nave – the area where the congregation sits.

Reredos (or Jesse Screen) – a screen or decoration behind the altar.

Rood screen – a screen dividing the nave from the chancel; the 'rood' is the crucifix on top of the screen.

Sanctuary – the area around the main altar within the communion rails.

Transept – the cross shaped part of the church between the nave and the chancel.

Vault – an arched, stone roof or a burial chamber.

Acknowledgements and notes

I have sought consent from the churches and abbeys to publish pictures I have taken on visits while researching this book. I have received kind words and encouragement from my requests for which I am very grateful. As well as urging you to visit these special places please consider donating to their funds as requested. In addition, many of them have excellent, informative guides at a very reasonable price.

I have included information about opening that I have been able to obtain. All of the churches were open and unlocked when I visited (except St Martin's, Wareham where a key is available close by) and if you visit in reasonable daylight hours I am sure there will be no problem.

Front cover: St Edwold's Church, Stockwood.
Rear cover: St Andrew's Church, Winterborne Tomson.
Above: Knowlton Church.
All photographs are by the author.